To Siobhan

Happy Birthday,

Love

Caroline
February 2003

Peter Brookes of THE TIMES

LITTLE, BROWN

A *Little, Brown* Book

First published in Great Britain in 2002 by Little, Brown

These cartoons first appeared in *The Times*
between May 1999 and June 2002

Copyright © Peter Brookes and Times Newspapers Ltd 2002

The moral right of the author has been asserted.

A CIP catalogue for this book is available from the British Library.

ISBN 0 316 72439 4

Typeset by M Rules in Bembo

Printed and bound in Italy

Little, Brown
An imprint of
Time Warner Books UK
Brettenham House
Lancaster Place
London WC2E 7EN

www.TimeWarnerBooks.co.uk

For Angela, Benjamin and William

NATO bombs Belgrade in the Kosovo War.

NATO bombs the Chinese Embassy in Belgrade, in error.

A deadlock is reached with Sinn Fein leader Gerry Adams over the decommissioning of IRA weapons in Northern Ireland.

President Jiang Zemin visits London; dissent on the controversial issue of human rights in Tibet is discouraged.

"NOW BE <u>REALLY</u> CLEVER, AND CLONE INTENSIVE CARE BEDS!"

... AND THE STREETS WERE PAVED WITH GOLD

The sources of Ken Livingstone's funding for his campaign to become London's Mayor are questioned.

Russia's new President Vladimir Putin is revealed to have a murky past.

"TRAGICALLY DIVIDED FOR YEARS...THE SOUTH BOOMING, THE NORTH POOR."

North Korea's economy collapses; South Korea prospers.

The Duke of Edinburgh (a.k.a. 'Phil the Greek') pronounces on GM foods.

Tony Blair is barracked by middle England at a Women's Institute conference.

Northern Ireland braces itself for the Protestant Orange Order's
controversial Drumcree march.

John Prescott announces a £180 billion ten-year plan to ease road congestion and boost public transport.

A memo is leaked, in which Tony Blair requests from his spin doctors eyecatching initiatives with which to be associated. Terrorists are freed from the Maze, quite possibly to reoffend.

THE SURVIVOR

Aboard the sunken submarine *Kursk* all are feared dead, along with *glasnost*.

ON HEARING THE SAD NEWS...

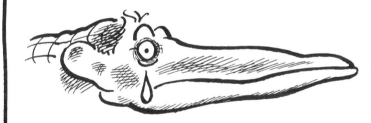

...THAT OUR MO IS QUITTING.

5 ix 00
Peter Brookes

Mo Mowlem resigns as Northern Ireland Secretary.

As he prepares for the General Election, the Tory leader William Hague reveals that as a youth he could down fourteen pints in a day.

The Dome continues to attract too few visitors and too much funding.

Foreign Secretary Robin Cook sends troops to Sierra Leone, raising fears of 'mission creep'.

A fuel crisis catches the Government unprepared.

The Sydney Olympic Games are fêted; the Government at home is battered by truckers.

William Hague exploits the populist tendency over Tony Martin's acquittal, the
paedophile protests in Portsmouth, and the fuel crisis.

Irish Republicans fire rockets at the MI6 headquarters, London. The Liberal-Democrat Party conference ends.

The Government basks in the reflected glory of Nelson Mandela's visit to the Labour Party conference.

On Ann Widdecombe's birthday the alcohol and irony flow freely on the conference platform at Bournemouth, as she announces a draconian new Tory drugs policy.

The shadow Cabinet queue up to admit to their past use of drugs, in a sudden policy climb-down.

The Bonn climate conference reaches an historic agreement, clearing the way
for the world to act on global warming. Tensions in the Middle East continue.

EGYPTIAN FREEZE...

Ehud Barak and Yasser Arafat fail in negotiations at a US-brokered summit in Egypt.

LEAVES ON THE LINE...

The Hatfield rail disaster

MIND THE GAP...

Fuel protesters make their moral case.

AMERICA DECIDES...

In the US presidential election the voters have a choice of candidates
George W. Bush and Al Gore.

Republicans and Democrats cannot agree who has won the presidential race.

"IF IT'S NOT ONE MAD COW, IT'S ANOTHER!"

Mad Cow Disease (BSE) rages. It is ten years since Baroness Thatcher was forced out of office.

The contents of the Queen's Speech come under scrutiny and are deemed to have been designed to suit a General Election in the spring.

SOLD DOWN THE RIVERDANCE...

The IRA continue to call the tune on arms decommissioning.

Sir Richard Branson's bid to replace Camelot in running the
National Lottery is denied.

George W. Bush, newly installed as US President, appoints some old favourites to his administration.

Bush announces his intention to ignore the Kyoto protocol.

THREATENED SPECIES

There is an oil spill off Scotland. Peter Mandelson faces pressure to resign (again) over the Hinduja brothers cash-for-passports affair.

Mandelson is finally forced to resign.

Steelmaker Corus to cut more than 6,000 jobs at steel plants in England and Wales.

Ariel Sharon is elected Prime Minister of Israel.

European monetary dis-union for Blair

Chancellor Gordon Brown produces an upbeat budget. William Hague appears to brand Britain 'a foreign land' flooded by asylum seekers.

Foot and mouth disease takes a heavy toll on British farmers' stock. The news is announced that the Russian spacecraft MIR could break up and land anywhere.

Blair is unable to conquer foot and mouth disease.

KEY:
☐ US
■ THEM

THE LEEDS TRIAL COLLAPSE & RETRIAL IS GREETED BY APPALLED OUTRAGE...

The trial of the Leeds United football players

Bush goes to great lengths to avoid saying 'sorry' for the US spy plane grounded in China.

ANOTHER PHOENIX, SURVIVOR OF MAY 3, FACING CERTAIN DEATH, JUNE 7...

Phoenix the calf is famously reprieved from foot-and-mouth slaughter. The
expected General Election date of May 3 is cancelled – but only until June 7.

U.S. ARMS INDUSTRY DIAGRAM: HOW SON OF STAR WARS WILL WORK.

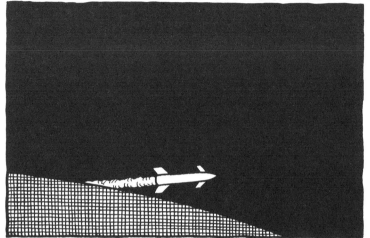

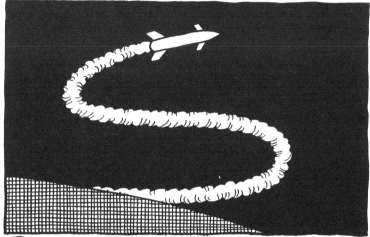

1 ENEMY MISSILE LAUNCHED...

2 U.K. RADAR TRACKS TRAJECTORY...

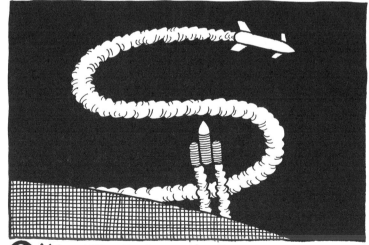

3 'KILLER VEHICLE' INTERCEPTS...

4 GEE, THAT IS **SO** BEAUTIFUL!

SCHOOL LAUNCH FOR ELECTION CAMPAIGN...

GEOGRAPHY DEPT.

HISTORY DEPT.

ENDORSEMENT

WILLIAM HAGUE

THE FINAL NAIL...

23 V 07
Peter Brookes

ENGLAND'S CAPTAIN ...

David Beckham sports a new mohican haircut. Blair reveals his euro-friendliness.

The 'Keep the Pound' campaign is not working for the Tories, in their bid for election success.

BACK AGAIN...

Blair wins the election by another landslide, eliciting comparisons to
the Thatcher years.

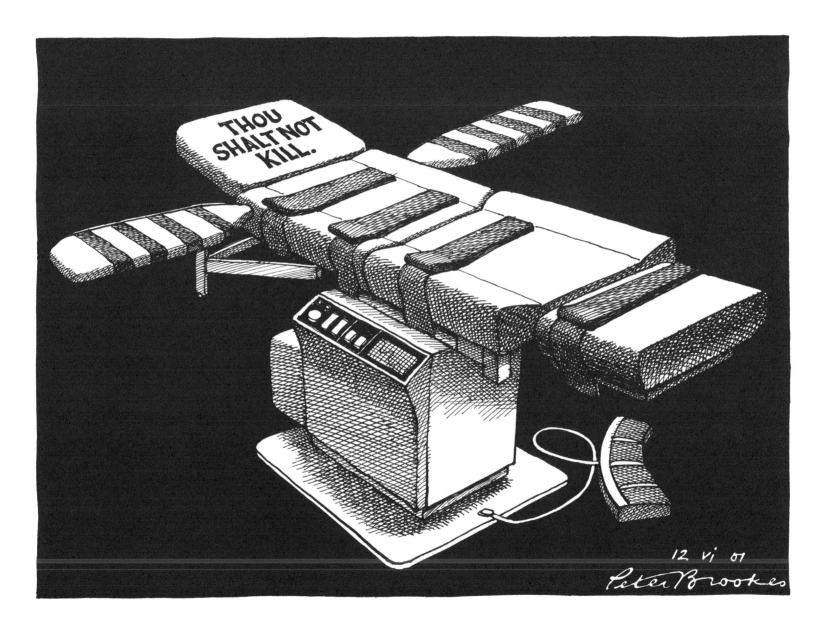

Timothy McVeigh, the Oklahoma bomber, is executed, media-style.

New Home Secretary David Blunkett oversees the demise of Paul Whitehouse,
Chief Constable of Sussex Police.

CENTRE COURT...

Slobodan Milosevic makes his first court appearance at The Hague.

1.

2.

3.

PAPER MILL

24 vii 01
Peter Brookes

4.

CLIMATE TALKS COMMUNIQUÉ

In the Tory leadership campaign, Iain Duncan Smith confronts his image problem.

New York and Washington are attacked.

Unnoticed amidst the September 11 fall-out, Iain Duncan Smith is elected as the new Tory leader.

15 ix 01

Peter Brookes after the photograph of St. Paul's Cathedral, the Blitz 1940.

Washington, after September 11 attack on the Pentagon

Back to work...

The coalition in the War against Terror is extremely fragile.

Blair embarks on thousands of air miles of shuttle diplomacy to shore up the alliance. Meanwhile, airlines are collapsing in the post–September 11 economic climate.

George W. Bush displays an injudicious choice of language whilst referring to the War on Terror.

Prince Edward's television production company, Ardent, breaches Royal Family guidelines by filming Prince William at the University of St Andrews.

BEFORE

AFTER

The US and the UK bomb Kabul, Afghanistan, already in ruins after twenty years of conflict with Russia and internal civil war.

"Martin McGuinness and I have held discussions with the IRA."
— Gerry Adams

Missed targets in Afghanistan, innocent civilians are killed.

Osama Bin Laden holds out.

British citizens fight for the Taliban.

Blair neuters the House of Lords.

Kabul returns to the twenty-first century, after the defeated Taliban flee.

Stephen Byers' spin doctor Jo Moore had infamously tried to use September 11 as a 'good day to bury bad news'. Byers refuses to sack her and problems mount for the Transport Secretary.

NHS TRANSPLANT SURGERY...

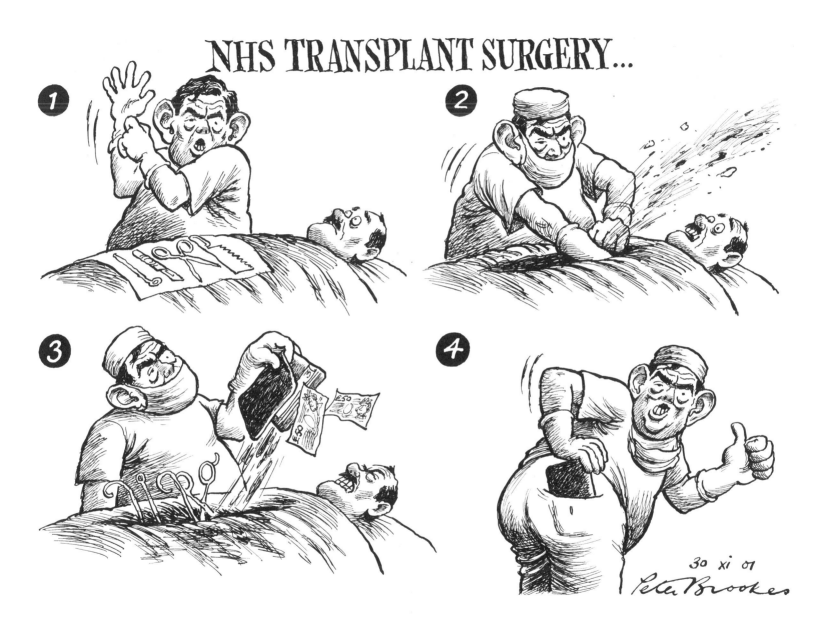

Gordon Brown announces higher taxes in order to increase spending on the NHS.

Bombing Afghanistan is deemed a military success, but no one knows where Bin Laden is hiding.

The rapturous launch of the euro

More commuter misery undermines Transport Secretary Stephen Byers.

Taliban prisoners, including Britons, are transported to Guantanamo Bay, Cuba, and are allegedly given harsh treatment. Meanwhile Gerry Adams and Martin McGuinness of Sinn Fein are given prime office space in St Stephen's Tower, House of Commons.

A flu epidemic threatens Britain, as Adams and McGuinness take up their new residence.

Mike Tyson is refused a license to box. The proposed military action by Bush against Iraq is claimed to be in breach of international law.

Enron, the largest company in the US, goes bust after accounting irregularities are uncovered on its balance sheets. Lord Wakeham, in Enron's pay, is forced to resign as chairman of the Press Complaints Commission.

ASYLUM SEEKERS U.K. CITIZENSHIP TEST. CAN YOU...

1 SPEND FOUR DAYS ON AN NHS TROLLEY?

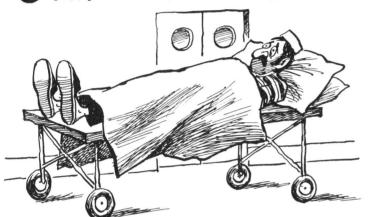

2 HANDLE A MOBILE PHONE MUGGING?

3 WAIT FOR A TRAIN WHICH NEVER COMES?

4 PUT UP WITH OUR POST?

THE GOONS...

Spike Milligan, the last of the Goons, dies, but memories of them live on.

Zimbabwe prepares for 'democratic' elections.

Dick Cheney, US Vice President, arrives at Downing Street for talks on possible
military action on Iraq.

The prospect of war with Iraq seems a doddle compared to solving the Israel–Palestine conflict.

Zimbabwe votes.

Yasser Arafat's headquarters are blockaded by Israeli forces, following a wave of Hamas suicide bombings.

Gordon Brown's Budget is seen to have done no harm to his political ambitions.

Voter apathy propels Jean-Marie Le Pen to second place in the first round of the French presidential elections. There are similar problems during the local elections in England.

Stairwell, Peckham

Peter Brookes
26 iv 02

'Not guilty' verdicts are announced in the Damilola Taylor murder case.

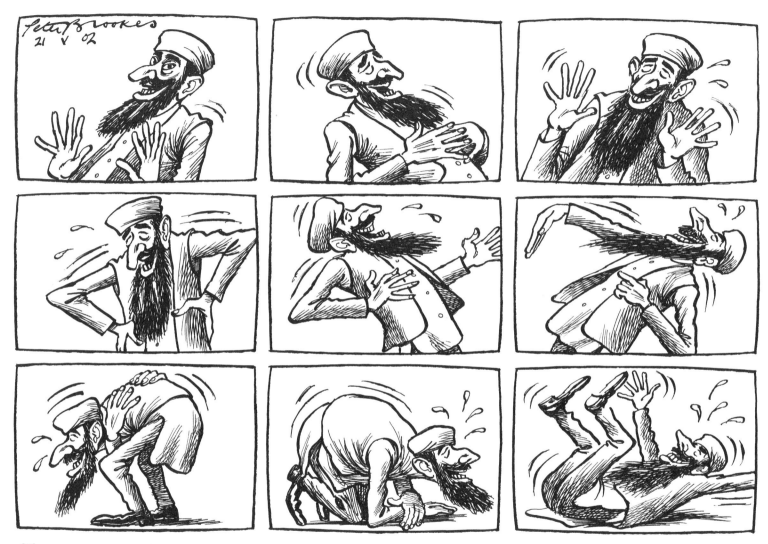

Latest bin Laden video received by Ministry of Defence & Royal Marines...

The Royal Marines commander in Afghanistan and the Ministry of Defence
are at loggerheads.

Tony Blair announces tough new measures against asylum seekers.

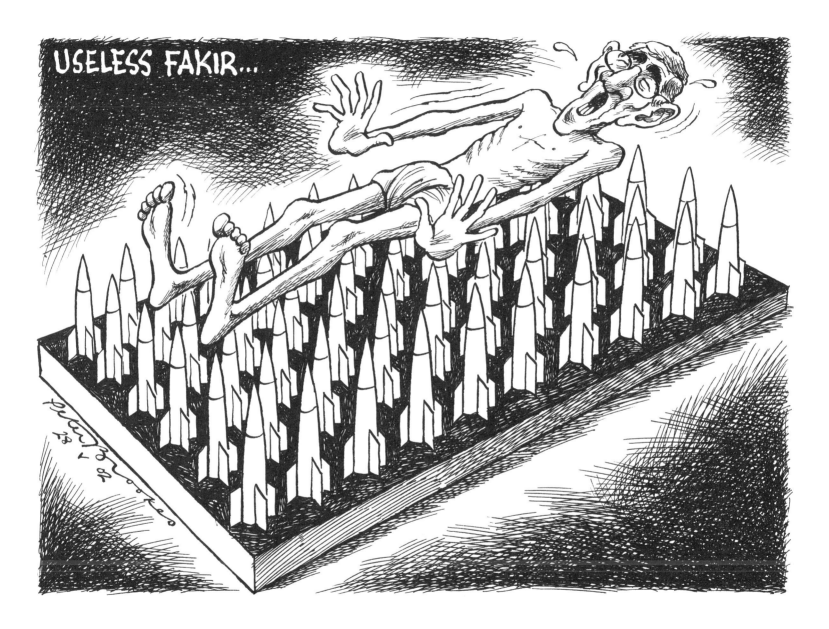

USELESS FAKIR...

Foreign Secretary Jack Straw visits India and Pakistan to ease tension over Kashmir, while Britain continues to sell arms to both sides. Pakistan tests out its nuclear weapons during his visit.

Stephen Byers resigns as Transport Secretary, and is replaced by Alistair Darling.

Spin fails to boost the besmirched standing of the Prime Minister.

Cherie Blair and Foreign Secretary Jack Straw voice concern for Palestinian suicide bombers, on the same day as nineteen Israelis are blown up.

Anti-Terror Wall, West Bank...

Israel constructs a barrier to deter the suicide bombers.

THE RAFT OF THE MOODUSA *by Géricow*

France bans British beef in the BSE crisis. Agriculture Minister Nick Brown
is all at sea.

"THOU ALL-DESTROYING BUT UNCONQUERING WHITE WHALE... TO THE LAST I GRAPPLE WITH THEE."
(AHAB, 'MOBY DICK')

General Pinochet recovers from an apparently debilitating illness remarkably quickly, on his release from Britain.

US presidential elections 2000

Home Secretary David Blunkett puts forward shorter sentencing proposals.

HISTORY...

1900s GREAT WAR 20s 30s 40s 50s 60s 70s 80s 90s

HER STORY...

1900s GREAT WAR 20s 30s 40s 50s 60s 70s 80s 90s

The death of the Queen Mother

STATE FUNERALS...

As the Queen Mother is buried, so are the aspirations for Palestine and Israel.